Matthew Hall

PEARSON
PUBLISHING

Saxon and Viking Britain

Stewart Ross

Illustrations by Lyndsay Crosbie and Julie Beer

ISBN 1 85749 093 2

Published Pearson Publishing, Chesterton Mill, French's Road, Cambridge CB4 3NP

First edition 1993
Reprinted 1999
Text © Stewart Ross, 1993

Contents

Rome

The Roman Empire

The Romans came from the city of Rome, in Italy. More than 2000 years ago they gradually **conquered** the rest of Italy.

They then went on to conquer other lands and peoples. They marched into France, Germany, Greece and Egypt – no one was strong enough to stop them. By the time of the birth of Jesus Christ, the Romans were the most powerful people in Europe.

The area they governed is known as the **Roman Empire**.

The Roman Empire at its largest

Roman Britain

Can you see the island of Britain (**Britannia**) on the map? It is at the very edge of the Roman Empire.

The Romans **invaded** Britannia in 43 AD. (This date is explained on the next page.) They conquered all England and Wales, but not Scotland. The Romans were brilliant soldiers, organisers and builders. They brought many advantages to the people of Britannia.

For a long time the country was peaceful and **prosperous**. Roman law kept people in order. The countryside was dotted with large houses. Fine towns with public baths and theatres were linked by excellent roads.

1 The end of Roman Britain

The Romans even built a large wall – **Hadrian's Wall** – right across the north of the country to keep out attackers.

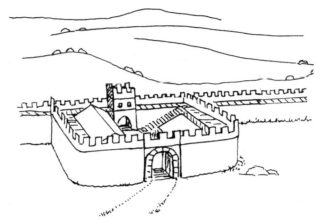

A fort on Hadrian's Wall

Time

Dates

Dates tell us when things happened. We arrange them around the time of the birth of Jesus Christ.

- Dates before this time are known as BC – **B**efore **C**hrist. They are counted *backwards*. For example 2000 BC came after 3000 BC.
- Dates after the birth of Christ are known as AD. This comes from the **Latin** (the language of the Romans) words **A**nno **D**omini, meaning 'the year of our Lord'. AD dates are counted *forwards*. So 150 AD was before 250 AD. The year we are in now is an AD date.
- If we are not sure of a date, we write a small c in front of it. The c stands for the Latin *circa*, meaning 'about'. 'c 340 BC' means 'about 340 years before the birth of Christ'.

Something to do

1 Colour the picture above.

2 Which was earlier:

    a 40 BC or 50 BC? _____

    b 200 AD or 300 AD?_____

    c 94 BC or 94 AD? _____

3 Write last year as an AD/BC date: _____

Centuries

The Romans were in Britain from 43 AD to c 410 AD. That is almost four hundred years, or four **centuries**. A century is a period of 100 years. The first (1st) century AD began on 1 January 1 AD and ended on 31 December 100 AD. The 2nd century AD went from 101 to 200, the 3rd century from 201 to 300, and so on.

Something to do

1 Give the dates of these AD centuries:

    a 2nd century___101___ to _____

    b 8th century_____ to _____

    c 18th century_____ to _____

    d 20th century_____ to _____

2 What century are we in now? _____

Barbarians!

The end of the Roman Empire

The Roman Empire was surrounded by jealous and warlike tribes. The Romans called these people **Barbarians**. The Barbarian tribes were always trying to break into the Roman Empire to get their hands on its wealth. One of the fiercest tribes were the **Vandals** – their name has come into our language. Do you know what we mean by a vandal? _____

_____

By about 400 AD the Romans could hold out no longer – the barbarians broke through. Rome ordered all its soldiers to return home. By 410 AD Britannia had been left to defend itself.

A valuable bar of lead made in Roman Britain

Rebellious mercenaries

Before the Roman soldiers left, Britannia had been attacked by bands of pirates from the north.

The Romans had paid **mercenaries** to protect the shores of Britannia. These mercenaries from northern Europe are known as Anglo-Saxons. In time, they brought their wives and families to live with them. When the Roman soldiers left, the Anglo-Saxons rebelled against the Britons. They conquered small **territories** for themselves.

What can you remember?

1   What language did the Romans use? _____

2   What did the Romans call people who lived outside their empire? _____

3   What does the word **conquer** mean? _____

4   What does Anno Domini mean? _____

5   Which years come first, AD or BC? _____

6   How many years are there in a century? _____

7   What did the Romans call Britain? _____

8   What is a mercenary? _____

9   Which mercenaries guarded Britannia's shores? _____

10   When did the last Roman soldiers leave Britain? _____

How do we know?

Sources

How do we know about the history of this time?

We learn about all history from **sources**. A source is anything which tells us about the past. Sources are also called **evidence**. School pupils usually find out about history from things like books, packs and videos. These are made by **historians** – people who study history.

Types of source

There are two types of historical source

1 **Original (or primary) sources**

   These come from the time we want to know about. For example, a description of Britain by the Roman writer Tacitus is an original source about Roman Britain, because he wrote it at the time. Original sources are the best way of finding out about the past.

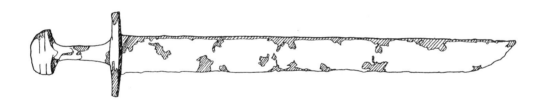

An Anglo-Saxon sword – this is original evidence about the Anglo-Saxons

Something to do

What can you learn about the Anglo-Saxons by looking at the sword in the picture above? (For example, it tells us that they knew how to make things out of metal.)

_____

_____

2 Secondary sources

These are usually books written by people who have studied original sources. They are a quick and easy way of finding out about the past. Most of this book is a secondary source.

Something to do

1 Explain the difference between an original and a secondary source, using your own words: _____

_____

_____

2 Is a video about the Anglo-Saxons an original source? yes/no

Original sources

Four types of original source about a **period** we want to know about are:

1 writing, such as newspapers, letters, diaries, poems or books

2 paintings, drawings, carvings, photographs and films

3 anything made, from pots and pans to temples or ships

4 the spoken word, *either* recorded *or* said by people who were alive at the time.

Historians use sources like detectives. Sources are *clues* about the past. They put together all the clues they can find to build up a picture of the past.

Something to do

Look carefully at the list of four types of original sources given above. *One of* these types cannot help us to find out about the Anglo-Saxons.

Write down which one you think it is (1, 2, 3, 4) _____ and say *why* you have given that answer:

_____

_____

Archaeology

Unfortunately, there are not that many Latin sources about Britain. And the early Anglo-Saxons wrote down very little. Because of this, much of what we know about this time comes from the buried remains of objects and buildings. Searching for this kind of evidence is known as **archaeology**.

Archaeologists digging for evidence about the past

Some Roman remains, such as roads, are quite easy to find. But archaeologists come across other remains, such as the walls of buildings and pottery, only by careful digging.

Something to do

1 Which of the types of source mentioned in the list on page 8 do you think would be the most useful? _____

   Why? _____

2 On a separate sheet of paper, make a list of objects which:

   a last a long time when they are buried (such as bones or pottery)

   b soon rot away in the ground (such as clothes).

   Which list do you think archaeologists, are most interested in, a or b?_____

   Explain why you gave that answer.

   _____

   _____

Invasion!

Invaders from Europe

When the Roman soldiers left, the **Romano-Britons** (Britons who had Roman lifestyles and customs) faced serious danger. Britannia was invaded by warriors and settlers from northern Europe and Scotland. They came first for **plunder**, then for land.

The Anglo-Saxon invasions

- **The Picts** attacked over Hadrian's Wall from Scotland. They did not conquer much of England for long.
- **The Angles** sailed from north Germany, Denmark, Norway and Sweden. They moved into north and east England. The region we now call East Anglia ('the place of the East Angles') is named after them. So is England itself. It means the 'land of the Angles' ('Angle-land').
- **The Saxons** invaded south and east England from Germany and Denmark. They gave their name to three areas of modern England: Middlesex 'the place of the middle Saxons'; Essex 'east Saxons'; and Sussex 'south Saxons'.
- **The Jutes** came from roughly the same areas as the Angles. Today there is still a region of Denmark called Jutland ('land of the Jutes'). The Jutes landed in Kent, Hampshire and the Isle of Wight.

To make things easier, we call all four groups simply Anglo-Saxons.

The Dark Ages

It is very difficult indeed to find out what was happening in Britain at this time. We have some ancient **accounts** of the Anglo-Saxon invasions. But only a few of them were written during the invasions themselves, and they are not very accurate.

Most of our evidence comes from archaeology. For example, archaeologists know what kind of jewelry the Anglo-Saxons wore. When they find this type of jewelry somewhere in Britain, they believe the invaders were there.

Other evidence for where the Anglo-Saxons went comes from cemeteries and the names of settlements. Because we know so little about this period of history, it is sometimes known as the **Dark Ages.**

An Anglo-Saxon bronze buckle

What can you remember?

1 What are the names of the four groups of people which attacked Britain when the Roman legions left?

   _____   _____

   _____   _____

2 Where in Europe did these people come from?

   a The Jutes _____ b   The Saxons _____

3 Name a part of England where:

   a The Saxons settled _____

   b The Angles settled _____

4 What do we mean by the 'Dark Ages'? _____

King Arthur

You have probably heard the stories of King Arthur and his Knights of the Round Table. They are some of the most famous **legends** in British history. We do not know who the real King Arthur was.

In the legends the king and his knights wear heavy **armour** like that worn after 1000 AD. But Arthur lived long before that. He was probably a famous Romano-British leader who fought against the Anglo-Saxon invaders in the fifth century.

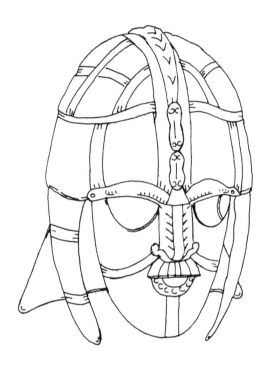

An Anglo-Saxon helmet

Ambrosius

The Anglo-Saxons took hundreds of years to conquer the whole of England. There were periods of peace and periods of war.

Sometimes the British drove back the invaders. In c 540 a Briton named Gildas wrote *The Ruin of Britain*. It is an account of the fighting in the early part of the fifth century. He said that a Romano-British leader named Ambrosius Aurelianus defeated the invaders at a place called Mons Badonicus.

Unfortunately, we know little else about Ambrosius or about his victory. But it does seem that the Britons put up a good fight.

What happened to the Britons?

By about 600 England had broken up into many small kingdoms. Some were Anglo-Saxon, others were still British. This map shows the most important kingdoms.

Britain in about 600

The Anglo-Saxon kingdoms were in the east and the British ones in the west. Over the next 200 years the Anglo-Saxons conquered all the remaining British kingdoms – *Dumnonia* (Cornwall), *Elmet and Rheged*. They did not conquer Wales or Scotland.

During many centuries of fighting a lot of Britons were killed. Others became slaves or fled to Wales or Scotland. But many ordinary people lived as they had always done, except that they now had Anglo-Saxon masters in place of British ones. The old **Celtic** and Romano-British **civilization** of Roman Britain slowly changed to an Anglo-Saxon civilization.

13

The New Kingdoms

The Anglo-Saxons were warlike people. They fought each other as well as the British. Some of the smaller Anglo-Saxon kingdoms, such as Essex and Kent, were conquered by the larger ones. By c 850 there were three important kingdoms – **Wessex**, **Mercia** and **Northumbria**.

Sometimes a very powerful king was known as the **Bretwalda**, meaning 'All-Britain-ruler'. Local kings accepted him as their overlord.

Gradually the whole of England was becoming one country again, as it had been in Roman times.

England in about 850

What can you remember?

Fill in the gaps in these sentences with the right words from the following list:

Deira   Ambrosius Aurelianus   Mercia   Bernicia   Gildas   Bretwaldas

1 _____ wrote *The Ruin of Britain* in the fifth century.

2 _____ was the large Anglo-Saxon kingdom in the middle of England.

3 The most powerful Anglo-Saxon kings were known as _____.

4 The small kingdoms of _____ and _____ became part of Northumbria.

5 _____ defeated the Anglo-Saxons at *Mons Badonicus*.

Something to do

1 Colour the map on page 13 and underline:

a   the British kingdoms in red and

b   the Anglo-Saxon kingdoms in blue.

2 Study the maps on pages 13 and 14. Can you find six independent kingdoms which existed in c 600 but not c 850?

_____   _____   _____

_____   _____   _____

Change and Continuity

Anglo-Saxon England – change ...

'Anglo-Saxon England' means England between c 450 and the arrival of the Normans in 1066 – a period of about 600 years.

During this time there were many changes. Kingdoms came and went; Christianity became the main religion; and by the ninth century the Anglo-Saxons were fighting for survival against new invaders – the Vikings. They introduced new ideas and customs to Anglo-Saxon England.

So it is not easy to say what Anglo-Saxon England was like.

People living in different parts of the country had different ways of doing things. And something that was true in the sixth century might not have been true 400 years later.

... and continuity

Continuity means continuing from one time to another. Historians think there was quite a lot of continuity between Roman England and Anglo-Saxon England.

Take Kent, for example:
- The Kingdom of Kent, the first Anglo-Saxon kingdom in England, covered the same area as a Roman district of government.
- People lived in the city of Canterbury right through the period of the Anglo-Saxon invasions.
- Christians have probably worshipped in Canterbury's church of St Martin since Roman times.

So perhaps the Anglo-Saxons took over Kent without destroying too much of what they found there.

Kings and coronations

The first Anglo-Saxon kings were successful war leaders who came to England with bands of warriors. The more successful they were, the more men joined them.

They spent much time fighting, plundering and feasting in large wooden halls. The Anglo-Saxon poem *Beowulf* talks of this sort of life. Later kings spent more time on government. The Witan (**council**) of about 35 advisors helped them.

The king and the Witan

Kings

- issued written laws
- ordered coins to be **minted**
- collected taxes
- issued **charters** giving away land or privileges
- led their armies in battle.

Offa, King of Mercia, built an enormous ditch to mark the boundary between his kingdom and Wales. **Offa's Dyke** still exists (see page 27). So that his **subjects** could see his importance, a new king began his reign with a **coronation**. By the tenth century coronations were complicated religious services. They gave the king God's special protection.

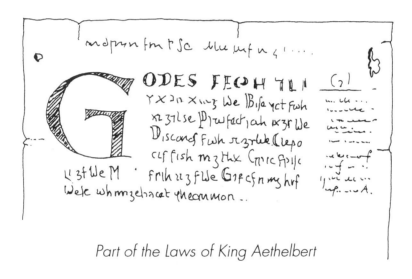

Part of the Laws of King Aethelbert

Shires

The later Anglo-Saxon kingdoms were very large, and by the eleventh century England had become one kingdom (this is explained in chapter 4.)

One king could not look after a large kingdom on his own. He divided it into **shires**. The modern word for a shire is a 'county'. Many modern counties are called shires, such as Hamp**shire** or York**shire**. A shire was named after its most important town. An **ealdorman** was in charge of each shire. Ealdorman was later shortened to 'earl', a title still used today. Harold, the last Anglo-Saxon king, was Earl of Wessex before he became king.

An ealdorman saw that the law was obeyed (there was a law court in each shire). He also led the men of his shire in battle and collected the king's taxes.

Later, kings put a **reeve** in charge of each shire. From 'shire-reeve' we get our word 'sheriff'.

Something to do

Find six counties which contain the word 'shire':

_____ _____ _____

_____ _____ _____

Hundreds and wappentakes

By the eleventh century each shire in Anglo-Saxon areas was divided into **hundreds**, and into **wappentakes** in Viking areas. A hundred was an area with about 100 peasant families living in it.

Taxes were collected in hundreds. In time of war each hundred had to provide soldiers for the king's army (the **fyrd**). There was a small law court in each hundred, too.

An Anglo-Saxon soldier

What can you remember?

Put a circle round the correct answer:

1 By 'Anglo-Saxon England' we mean the period:

    c 410 – 900
    400 – 1000   c 450 – 1066

2 Between the Roman and Anglo-Saxon periods there was quite a lot of:

    complexity   continuity   continental

3 The king's council was known as the:

    fyrd   ealdorman   Witan

4 An Anglo-Saxon shire was divided into:

    peasants   reeves   hundreds

5 An ealdorman was in charge of a:

    shire   wappentake   coronation

Towns and trade

Anglo-Saxon England was a wealthy kingdom. New towns sprang up and old ones grew bigger. They were centres of trade and **manufacture**. Some towns were fortified against attacks by the Vikings. These places were known as **burghs**.

London was by far the biggest town, with a **population** of about 20 000. Winchester grew, too, reaching a population of about 10 000. Other towns were no larger than modern villages, with populations of about 2000.

Several busy ports, such as Southampton, Dover, London, Ipswich and Whitby, grew rich. They shipped English goods abroad, particularly wool, and brought in foreign goods, such as wine and silver.

A silver penny of King Offa of Mercia

Food and health

Most Anglo-Saxons lived on farms or in small villages. They ate plenty of meat and bread, and drank a lot of beer. Some historians believe the Anglo-Saxons were better fed, taller and healthier than people living in later centuries.

Writers ...

Priests were just about the only people in Anglo-Saxon England who knew how to read and write. Because the **Christian church** looked after education and learning, many books were religious. The Bible and stories of the saints were the most popular.

The two books which most interest historians are:
1 *The **Ecclesiastical** [Religious] History of the English People*. This was written in Latin in the eighth century by a **monk** named Bede. He tells the story of the Anglo-Saxons from their arrival in Britain to his own time. It is a very valuable original source for that period of history.
2 *The Anglo-Saxon Chronicle*, another history of the Anglo-Saxons, written in their own language. It was put together by different monks for 200 years.

All books were rare and precious. Each one had to be written out by hand, taking many weeks. The margins and some letters were decorated with fantastic designs and drawings.

A capital letter from an Anglo-Saxon Bible made at Lindisfarne

Something to do

Colour this picture. The artist who drew it used different reds, blues, greens, gold and white.

...and artists

As well as books, the Anglo-Saxons created many other beautiful things.

They wrote poetry and made music. Their craftworkers produced wonderful jewelry, **tapestry** and carvings. Much Anglo-Saxon work has been lost. From what remains it is clear that they were a most talented people.

King Alfred's Jewel

Religion

Pagan gods

Christians called the Anglo-Saxon invaders **pagans**, meaning they did not believe in the Christian god. Like the Celts and early Romans, the Anglo-Saxons worshipped many gods. Their wooden temples and countryside **shrines** were destroyed or forgotten long ago. But the names of four of their gods are remembered in days of the week:

Tuesday – the day of the god *Tiw*

Wednesday – *Woden's* day

Thursday – *Thunor's* day

Friday – *Frig's* day

Even the name of Easter, the Christians' most important festival, comes from a pagan goddess, *Eostre*.

The making of Christian England

300 years after the Anglo-Saxon invasions, England was a Christian country. How did this happen?

1   There were some Christian churches in Roman Britain. A few survived the pagan invasions. One piece of evidence for this comes from place names. The Latin word *ecclesia* means a church. In Roman times there were Christian churches at places with names such as Eccles, Eccleston or Eccleshill. These places could be found in Anglo-Saxon times and still exist today.

2   Christian **missionaries** came to England from the ancient Christian churches in Ireland and Scotland.

3   Other missionaries came to England from France.

4   A third group of missionaries came from the Christian headquarters in Rome. Led by St Augustine, they landed in Kent in 597. They converted King Aethelred and went on to spread the Christian faith to other kingdoms.

Whitby

In this higgledy-piggledy way the English were converted to Christianity. It took a long time and was not done easily. One of the problems the priests had to sort out was that the old church of Ireland and Scotland was different from the Roman church. For example, they celebrated Easter at different times. In the end the leaders of the two churches met at Whitby in 663. They agreed that the whole English church should follow the ways of Rome.

St Martin's Cross, an early Christian carving from the Scottish Island of Iona

Monasteries and bishops

The English church became very powerful.
- Wealthy Christians gave it lots of land and money.
- Because priests controlled education and learning, kings needed them to help with the government. There were always **bishops** on the Witan.

The country was divided up into dioceses, each with its own bishop. He looked after the priests and people in his area. Many monasteries were founded. They had their own lands. The monks and nuns who lived in them enjoyed a good life. The Christian church was richer and more important than it is today.

King Alfred

Alfred was king of Wessex from 871 to 899. He was one of those lucky people who are good at just about everything. Because he was a skilled and brave soldier, a good organiser and a scholar, he is sometimes called 'Alfred the Great'.

In 878 Alfred defeated the Vikings in battle and persuaded their leader, Guthrum, to become a Christian (see page 34). He then strengthened his kingdom by improving the army, setting up burghs (see page 19) and building up a fleet of ships.

As well as all this, he found time to issue a code of laws and **translate** Latin books into Anglo-Saxon.

His court became very famous and people came from far and wide to visit it.

What can you remember?

Fill in the gaps in these sentences with the right words from the following list:

    wool   pagans   Bede   St Augustine   Thunor

1 The Anglo-Saxons shipped _____ abroad.

2 Thursday is named after the god _____.

3 _____ wrote an important history of the English people.

4 _____ came from Rome to convert the _____.

The Anglo-Saxon Legacy

The English language

A **legacy** is something left behind. The most important legacy from the Anglo-Saxons is English – the language of England.

Modern English (which we use) began with the language used by the Anglo-Saxons (sometimes called Old English). Although it has changed a lot since then, you will be able to recognise some Anglo-Saxon words. They had one letter (þ) for the 'th' sound, and they wrote 'a' and 'e' together, like this: æ.

Anglo-Saxon Word	Modern English Word
ond	and
wiþ	with
broþur	brother
ofer	over
was	was
lond	land
þær	there

The names of all sorts of everyday things (for example house, dog, tree, cow, road) come from the Anglo-Saxon.

Literature

As well as the Anglo-Saxon language itself, we also have fine **literature** from that period. Some works, like the poem *Beowulf*, are in Anglo-Saxon; other works, like Bede's *History*, are in Latin. Today not many people can read the original works, but we can enjoy them in translation.

In one of his most famous pieces of writing, Bede says that our life on earth is like a sparrow flying through a king's hall:

Within the hall there is a warm fire; outside the winter storms rage. The sparrow flies in at one door and out of another. Inside he is safe and comfortable; but he soon vanishes again into the darkness from which he came. This is like our life. We have no idea where we came from or where we go when we die.

[Adapted]

Place names

Hundreds of place names come from Anglo-Saxon settlements. The three most common are:

1 **–ing** from *ingas*, meaning a group of people. For example,

Tooting = 'Tota's people'

Reading = 'Reada's people'

2 **–ham** meaning a settlement or home. For example,

Horsham = the places where horses were kept

Aldenham = the old settlement

3 **–tun** meaning a farm or village. For example,

Sutton = south farm (– tun usually changed to –ton)

Stretton = village on a street or road

Sometimes two of these are joined together. For example,

Nottingham = the settlement (–ham) of Snot's people (–ing)

Allington = the farm (–tun) of Aella's people (–ing).

Something to do

1 Look at a modern map of England. Try to find more Anglo-Saxon place names. Write them down and next to them say whether they are –ing, –ham or –tun words, or a mixture of two of them:

_____

_____

_____

_____

_____

2 Mark in the names you have found on this map of Britain. This will tell you in
which regions the Anglo-Saxons settled.

The Christian Church

There are many different religions in England today. How many can you think of? _____ _____ _____

_____ _____ _____

Christianity is still the largest. And some of the dioceses set up by the Anglo-Saxons still exist – Canterbury, York, Winchester, London, Hereford, Worcester.

After the Whitby meeting there was one church organisation for all the English kingdoms. This helped later *Bretwaldas* to bring the whole country under one government.

For these reasons Christianity is a key legacy from the Anglo-Saxon period.

Buildings

The Anglo-Saxons built mainly in wood, so most of their houses, castles and churches disappeared long ago. However, you can still see the remains of Offa's Dyke.

Offa's Dyke

A few stone buildings remain, too. The picture on page 28 shows a tower which the Anglo-Saxons worked on from the seventh to the eleventh centuries.

The Anglo-Saxon church tower at Monkwearmouth

Works of art

Many smaller things made by the Anglo-Saxons have survived. They are an important part of our artistic **heritage**. They include weapons, jewels, books, carvings and paintings.

The finest collection was uncovered by archaeologists at Sutton Hoo in Suffolk. They dug under a mound of earth and found a ship filled with treasure. It belonged to an Anglo-Saxon king and was buried when he died in the seventh century. There were weapons and armour, spoons, dishes, bowls, coins and wonderful jewelry.

This **clasp** was made of gold and decorated with coloured glass and red garnet stones.

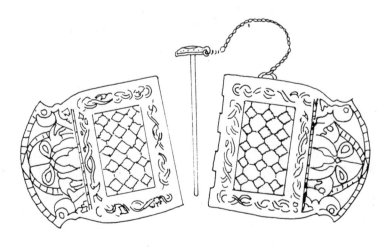

A clasp found at Sutton Hoo

Something to do

1 Colour the picture of the clasp on the previous page, showing how it might have looked when it was new.

2 Design your own piece of jewelry in Anglo-Saxon style;

What can you remember?

1 What does –ham mean?

_____

2 Name two modern dioceses which were set up in Anglo-Saxon times:

_____

_____

3 Draw the Anglo-Saxon letter which we write as th: _____

4 What was found at Sutton Hoo? _____

_____

5 What do we mean by our 'artistic heritage'? _____

_____

_____

6 Why have most Anglo-Saxon buildings disappeared?

_____

_____

Peril from the North

'Pagan Men'

The *Anglo-Saxon Chronicle* for 793 reads:

This year began with awful signs in Northumbria. The people were terrified by huge whirlwinds and flashes of lightning, and fire-breathing dragons flew through the air. Then came a terrible famine. Finally, on 8th June, pagan men attacked God's church at Lindisfarne. They slaughtered the monks and carried away treasure. [Adapted]

What on Earth was going on?

The writer talked about 'signs' because he did not believe that a terrible attack by 'pagan men' could have happened without a warning from God. The 'pagan men' were Vikings. The destruction of the Lindisfarne monastery was their first important raid on Anglo-Saxon England.

Who were the Vikings?

The Vikings were the people of Scandinavia. Most came from Norway and Denmark. From the late eighth century onwards they invaded Britain many times. Eventually many of them settled here. The Anglo-Saxon way of life survived, but the Vikings changed it quite a lot.

A map showing the Viking raids and important voyages

From the map on page 30, you will see that the Vikings sailed not only to Britain, but to Ireland and other countries as well.

Something to do

Write down the modern names of six countries which the Vikings reached:

_____ _____ _____

_____ _____ _____

And the modern names of three countries they came from:

_____ _____ _____

Why?

- The Vikings first came to England in bands of warriors. Like the Anglo-Saxons 350 years before them, they were looking for **loot**. The easiest thing to seize was treasure. After one quick raid they could sail home with a fortune in gold, silver and jewels. They also took things they could sell easily, such as cattle and captives, who were sold as slaves.
- Later, Vikings came in greater numbers, bringing their families with them. As well as loot, they wanted land to settle on. There was not much wrong with the land back home. There was just not enough of it for everyone. Viking families came to England to begin new lives in a rich and fertile country.

The sort of countryside from which the Vikings came

The first raids

The Vikings who attacked northern England were mostly from Norway. The Danes plundered further south. Sometimes warriors from Sweden came too. Norway, Denmark and Sweden are together known as **Scandinavia**.

The Norwegians arrived first. Christian monks had built monasteries on islands and other remote sites around the coasts of the British Isles. Lindisfarne was one of these quiet and peaceful places. Over the years the monasteries filled with valuable works of art – just the sort of thing the Vikings were looking for.

Lindisfarne monastery was plundered in 793, Jarrow in 794 and the Scottish monastery of Iona in 795. Meanwhile, other Vikings were raiding Kent and Sussex in the south of the country. After this, Viking raids died down for a while.

A Viking warrior

Something to do

Think about these four points, then answer the following questions:

- The best source of information about the Viking raids comes from Anglo-Saxon writings.
- Almost all Anglo-Saxon writing was done by monks.
- The Vikings were pagans.
- The first places the Vikings attacked were monasteries.

1 Why do you think Anglo-Saxon histories have nothing good to say about the Vikings?

_____

_____

2 Why do we have to be careful when using Anglo-Saxon sources about the Vikings?

_____

_____

Raids on the south

Serious Viking raids began again in the 830s. This time most of the attackers came from Denmark to the south of England.

They raided the Isle of Sheppey in 835. Seven years later they sacked London and Rochester. In 851 they attacked London again and sacked Canterbury.

Settlers

In the middle of the ninth century Viking **strategy** changed. In 865 they landed with a 'Great Army' to conquer England. Six years later the invaders were joined by a 'Great Summer Army'. Boatloads of settlers followed the soldiers to England.

The invaders defeated the Mercians and Northumbrians, and Viking families began to set up home in those kingdoms.

4 The Vikings

Of the three large Anglo-Saxon kingdoms, only Wessex survived. King Alfred overcame the Danes at Edington in 878 and made treaties with them:

- King Guthrum, the Danish leader, became a Christian.
- The Danes agreed to keep to the east of a line running across England from London to Chester. The frontier between the Danes and the English followed the old Roman road called Watling Street. The Danish land became known as the **Danelaw**, because the people there lived under Danish, not English law.

Anglo-Saxon and Viking Britain

Wessex fights back

Alfred was **succeeded** by very able sons and grandsons:

Edward the Elder	Reigned 899 to 924 (usually written 899–924)
Athelstan	924–39 (no need to repeat the first 9)
Edmund	939–46
Eadred	946–55

These kings of Wessex defeated the Vikings in many battles and reconquered the whole of England.

By the time of King Eadred and his son Edgar (957–75), the kings of Wessex ruled over all England. From this time onwards England was a single kingdom.

The return of the Danes

The Viking attacks had not finished.

During the reign of Edgar's son Aethelred (978–1016), the Danes raided England time and again. The king paid them money to go away. This money was known as **danegeld** (Dane + *geld*, meaning money). When they knew about this, the Danes returned to get more money!

Aethelred was followed by the only Danish king of all England, Cnut (1016–35). (There is more about Cnut on pages 43 and 44.)

After Cnut came Anglo-Saxon kings. But they did not last long. The last, King Harold, was killed by Norman invaders at the Battle of Hastings in 1066 and the long line of Anglo-Saxon kings came to an end.

The death of Harold at Hastings, from the Bayeaux Tapestry

4 The Vikings

What can you remember?

Fill in the gaps in these sentences with the right words from the following list:

Edgar   Danelaw   Aethelred   Lindisfarne   loot

1 The first Vikings came to England in search of _____ .

2 King _____ paid the Danes to leave England.

3 _____ became King of England in 957.

4 The _____ was to the east of Watling Street.

5 The Vikings attacked _____ monastery in 793.

Something to do

1 Colour and label the picture on page 35.

2 Give two reasons why the Vikings came to England:

   _____

   _____

3 On a separate piece of paper, draw a picture of the Viking attack on Lindisfarne.

4 Explain how Wessex was able to conquer the kingdoms of Mercia and Northumbria:

   _____

   _____

   _____

   _____

Sailors and Settlers

The Viking world

Many people think of the Vikings as just bloodthirsty warriors. It is true that some of them were very bloodthirsty. But they were not simply fighters and murderers.

They were also
- sailors and explorers
- craftsmen and artists
- poets and song-writers
- manufacturers and merchants.

They settled in many parts of Europe, bringing fresh ideas and energy. The empire they conquered in north-west Europe lasted for hundreds of years.

Viking warships

Viking ships were the best of their time.

A Viking warship

Warships (known as **longships**) like the one above were made of wooden planks which curved up to a point at each end. The ships were broad and flat in the middle. This meant that they could sail in very shallow water. They were steered with an oar at the stern.

The English were surprised to find Viking raiders sailing far up rivers where other ships could not go.

Longships were driven by sails or oars. With brightly painted shields hanging over the sides, they looked very frightening. Smaller ships carried about 30 men. The larger ones could hold many more than this, as well as horses.

Merchant ships

Viking warships were ideal for raiding up rivers and along the coast. But they were not so good for carrying loads or making long voyages in the open sea.

For this kind of work the Vikings used broader ships with decks, like the one in the picture below.

Viking merchant ship

As you can see, these ships held a lot of **cargo**. They were not as fast as longships. In rough weather the crew of both longships and merchant ships got wet and cold.

Something to do

Colour and label the picture of *either* the Viking longship *or* the Viking merchant ship.

Land-hunters

This map shows some of the amazing voyages made by Viking sailors.

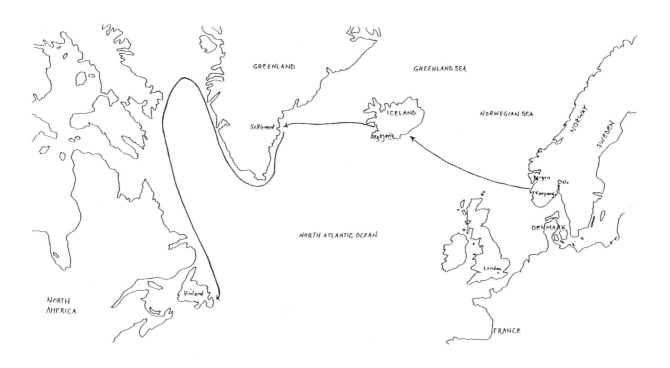

Where the Vikings explored

They were made by men and women looking for new places to live. As well as travelling down to the British Isles, they also sailed west into the North Atlantic.

- In the 860s they found the uninhabited island of Iceland. By the early tenth century they had settled there.
- Later in the century Eirik the Red (he had red hair and a red beard) got lost at sea and landed in *Groenland*, which was also uninhabited. Although it was a desolate place, Eirik called it *Groenland* (Greenland) to make it sound more attractive.
- Shiploads of Vikings went to live in Greenland.
- In about 985 the sailor Bjarni sighted America when he was trying to reach Greenland. He told other Vikings what he had seen. Leif the Lucky (son of Eirik, sometimes called Leif Eiriksson) went to have a look at the new land for himself. He called it Vine-land or Vinland, after the wild grapes he found growing near the shore.

- A few Vikings went to live in Vinland, but they did not survive for very long. Eirik's discovery was soon forgotten.
- It was another 500 years before Europeans saw America again.

What can you remember?

Complete these sentences:

1 Viking warships were also known as _____ .

2 They were steered by an _____ .

3 Eirik the Red discovered _____ .

4 The Viking name for America was _____ .

5 The name of the first Viking to land in America was _____ .

Houses

Viking houses were made of material they found all around them. In the north, where there were not many trees, they used stones and earth. In England the houses were made of wood.

First they put up a wooden frame. For the walls they used planks or sticks woven together. The roof was thatched. There was usually only one door and no windows. To let the smoke of the fire out, they left a hole in the roof. The insides of these houses must have been dark and smokey.

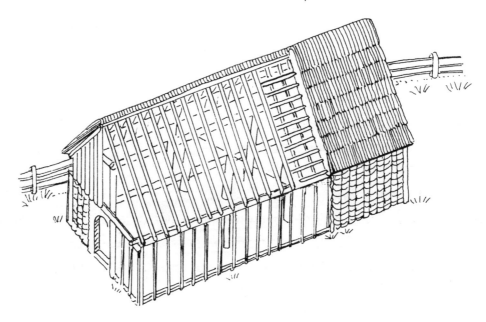

How a Viking house was made

Home life

Some Viking women went with the men on raids and adventures. Eirik the Red's daughter led an expedition to Vinland. But mostly Viking women were expected to stay at home. They looked after the children, did the cooking and made clothes.

Here is a picture of a woman at work inside a Viking house.

Something to do

Colour this picture and label these things: wooden bucket, fire, cooking pot, wooden spoon, ladle, wooden bowls, woman making bread, candle, chopping board and knife.

Artists and craftsmen

The Vikings were very creative. They decorated everyday things, such as swords and cups, with beautiful patterns often using snake and dragon shapes.

A metal Viking cup

They were fine carvers in wood and stone and loved poetry. In the eleventh century their poets began to write history in **sagas**. These were long poems, full of adventure, boasting and glory. They are fun to read. But they are difficult to use as sources because they don't always tell the truth!

Religion

The pagan Vikings

The Vikings who came to England were pagans. Like the Anglo-Saxons, they had many gods.

When heroes died, the Vikings believed their souls went to a great hall (called *Valholl*) in the palace of the god Odin. Here they enjoyed magnificent feasts. Odin's female servants, known as the *Valkyrie*, chose the men who were to die in battle, and then took them to *Valholl*.

Because of this, warriors were buried with all the possessions they might need in the next world. These burial places are wonderful sources of information for archaeologists.

Odin and Thor

Odin was described as *the father of all the gods who rules all things*.

There are many stories about Odin. One says that he rode an eight-legged horse. Another tells how he stole a magic drink, made out of honey and the blood of a murdered man. He gave it to favoured men to make them into poets.

Thor was another important Viking god. He was tremendously strong. At one feast he was said to have eaten an ox and eight salmon, and drunk a whole barrel of **mead**.

Thor's weapon was a huge hammer (named *Mjollnir*). The Vikings believed that thunder was the sound of Thor beating his hammer. Once *Mjollnir* was stolen and Thor had to dress up as the goddess of love (*Freyja*) to get it back!

Conversion

The English Vikings soon converted to Christianity. They were not all happy about this change. This piece of Viking silver work shows how some of the Vikings tried to keep in with both Christianity and paganism.

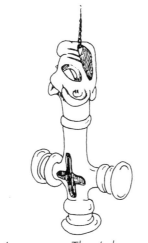

A cross or Thor's hammer?

Cnut

Cnut (who is sometimes called Canute) was the most famous Viking king of this period. He was the son of Sweyn, King of Denmark, and invaded England with his father in 1013.

The next year Sweyn died and the 18-year-old Cnut went home. He returned with three great Viking leaders, defeated the English leader Edmund 'Ironside' and was made king of all England.

In 1018 he became king of Denmark and in 1028 he conquered Norway. This made him the most powerful king in northern Europe.

Cnut is remembered as a skilful ruler. He got on well with both the English and the Vikings, and prevented squabbles between them. He was also a keen Christian. The church liked this and gave him its support.

Cnut was a wise king, too. There is a legend, which you may know, that Cnut's followers thought he was so great that he could tell the sea what to do. To show them how silly they were, Cnut stood on the shore and ordered the tide not to come in. It did, and he got his feet wet!

What can you remember?

Fill in the gaps in these sentences with the right words from the following list:

Thor   *Mjollnir*   *Valholl*   sagas   wood

1   The god _____ had a hammer named _____ .

2   The gods lived at _____ .

3   In England Viking houses were made of _____ .

4   Viking _____ are long poems about the adventures of great men.

Something to do

1   On a separate piece of paper, draw or paint a picture of *Valholl*.

2   Give four reasons why Cnut was thought to be a great king:

    a   _____

    b   _____

    c   _____

    d   _____

3   On a separate piece of paper, draw and label a piece of evidence which shows that some Christian Vikings did not forget about their pagan beliefs.

The Viking Legacy

What happened to the Vikings?

In time, the Vikings who settled in England accepted many of the ways of the Anglo-Saxons. They became Christians, their land was divided into shires and wappentakes, and they came under the same system of law as the Anglo-Saxons.

English and Vikings **intermarried** and the differences (such as language and customs) between them slowly disappeared.

One country

The most important effect of the Viking invasions was that England became a single country. As we have seen, this happened in two stages. Firstly, the Vikings overcame Mercia and Northumbria to create the Danelaw, and secondly Wessex conquered the Danelaw.

The shires in the eleventh century

Something to do

The map on the previous page shows the shires and main towns of England in the eleventh century. Using a modern map of England, find:

1 Three modern cities today which are not on the eleventh-century map:

_____ _____ _____

2 Three modern counties which did not exist in the eleventh century:

_____ _____ _____

Other effects

- The English were badly shaken up by the Viking invasions. Many religious writers believed that the attacks were a punishment from God for their bad behaviour.
  One result of this was **reform** of the Anglo-Saxon church in the tenth century. This was led by three bishops: Dunstan, Aethelwold and Oswald.
  A new way of organising life in the monasteries was introduced to England from Europe. It was known as the **Benedictine Rule**.
- The Viking settlements brought England closer to Scandinavia (see page 32). In 1066 King Harold had to fight against Scandinavian invaders as well as the Normans from France.
- The wars against the Vikings were very expensive. So was the payment of *Danegeld*. Kings collected more taxes from their people. This probably made ordinary farmers poorer than they had been before the Vikings came.

A copy of a tenth-century drawing of St Dunstan at the feet of Christ

Something to do

1 Colour and label the picture of Christ and St Dunstan.

2 Say why you think the artist made Dunstan so small and Jesus so big:

_____

Language

The languages of the Anglo-Saxons and Vikings were quite similar. It is possible that the two people could just about understand each other.

Many Scandinavian words came into English. The most important were *they, them,* and *their*. We also use other Scandinavian names every day: leg, egg, take, lake, skin, die, sale and wrong are just a few.

Place names

Many place names come from Viking settlements. The four most common are:
* **– by** meaning a farm or village. For example,
    Denby = 'Danes village' and Coningsby = 'the king's village'
* **– toft** meaning a home. For example,
    Bratoft = 'broad home' and Nortoft = 'north home'
* **– thwaite** meaning a meadow or clearing. For example,
    Applethwaite = 'apple-tree clearing' and Braithwaite = 'broad clearing'
* **– thorpe** meaning a small village. For example,
    Grassthorpe = 'grassy village' and Alethorpe = 'Ali's village'.

Something to do

1 Try to find some more Scandinavian place names on a map of modern England. Write them down and next to them say whether they are –by, –toft, –thwaite or –thorpe words:

_____

_____

_____

2 Copy or trace the outline map on page 26. On it mark in the Scandinavian names you have found. This will tell you in which regions the Vikings settled.

4 The Vikings

What can you remember?

1 List four effects of the Viking invasions:

_____

_____

_____

_____

2 What do these Scandinavian words mean?

a *thwaite* _____

b *toft* _____

c *thorpe* _____

3 Write down six English words which come from Scandinavia:

_____ _____ _____

_____ _____ _____

Answers

Note: Children may need help with the words in bold type.

Page 4: 2 a = 50 BC, b = 200 AD, c = 94 BC. Page 5: 1 a =200, b = 701 – 800, c = 1701 – 1800, d = 1901 – 2000. Page 6: 1 = Latin, 2 = Barbarians, 3 = attack and defeat, 4 = year of our Lord, 5 = BC, 6 = 100, 7 = Britannia, 8 = someone who fights for money, 9 = Anglo-Saxons, 10 = c 410 AD. Page 8: 2.= No, 4. Page 9: 1 = 1, 2 = a. Page. 11: 1 = Picts, Angles, Saxons, Jutes, 2 a = Denmark/Jutland, b = Germany and Denmark, 3 a = south and east, b = north and east, 4 = difficult to know what happened then. Page 15: 1 = Gildas, 2 = Mercia, 3 = Bretwaldas, 4 = Deira, Bernicia, 5 = Ambrosius Aurelianus. Page 19: 1 = c 450 – 1066, 2 = continuity, 3 = Witan, 4 = hundreds, 5 = shire. Page 23: 1 = wool, 2 = Thunor, 3 = Bede, 4 = St Augustine, pagans. Page 29: 1 = a settlement or home, 2 = any 2 from the list on page 27, 3 = Þ, 4 = a buried ship full of treasure, 5 = the works of art we have inherited from the past, 6 = made of wood. Page 36: 1 = loot, 2 = Aethelred, 3 = Edgar, 4 = Danelaw, 5 = Lindisfarne. Page 40: 1 = longships, 2 = oar, 3 = Greenland, 4 = Vinland, 5 = Leif the Lucky. Page 44: 1 = Thor, Mjollnir, 2 = Valholl, 3 = wood, 4 = sagas. Page 48: 1 = eg England became one country, new words into English, reform of the church, farmers poorer, 2 a = meadow or clearing, b = home, c = small village.